COLOR
OYSTER BAY

BY
JAKE ROSE

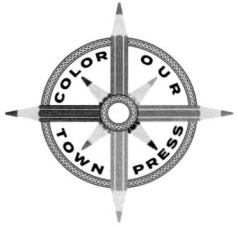

Color Our Town Press
200 E 71 Street
New York, NY 10021
www.colorourtown.com

ISBN 978-1-948286-34-3

Printed in USA

Cover designed by Jake Rose, Ivan Myerchuk, and Brenda Zabala.
Line illustrations by Ivan Myerchuk and Jake Rose.
Back cover art by Brenda Zabala

WELCOME TO HISTORIC OYSTER BAY

When I served in the United States Congress, I took great pride in recognizing that much of our national history was forged locally–on the streets of Oyster Bay.

Here in our waterfront hamlet, Washington's spy ring operated out of Raynham Hall. Then, of course, there is the relationship between our community and President Theodore Roosevelt. The Sagamore Hill National Historic Site is a quick drive from town. On the way, you can visit Roosevelt's gravesite and the adjoining Theodore Roosevelt Audubon Sanctuary. The building housing Roosevelt's summer executive offices still stands proudly at the intersection of East Main and South streets. And so much more!

OYSTER BAY HAS MADE MORE RECENT HISTORY.

In the past year, our downtown has blossomed with new restaurants, a brewery, an artisanal chocolatier, and yes, what every downtown needs, a bookshop. You can stroll passed new age shops and historic buildings; you can experience past and future in the lively downtown I'm proud to call home.

STEVE ISRAEL

Owner, Theodore's Books & Former Member of Congress

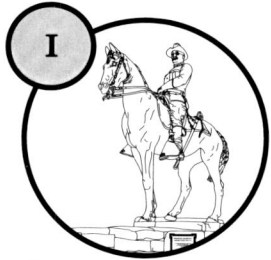

1 Theodore Roosevelt Statue

2 Moore's Building/ Wild Honey

3 Sagamore Hill

4 Coe Hall

5 Snouder's Corner Drug Store

6 Raynham Hall

7 Theodore's Books

8 Shops of Oyster Bay

9 Bonanza Stand

10 2 Spring

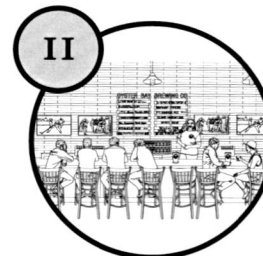

11 Oyster Bay Brewing Company

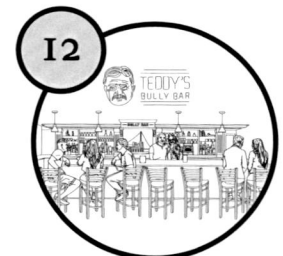

12 Teddy's Bully Bar

13 Oyster Bay Railroad Museum

14 Oyster Bay Historical Society

15 Oyster Bay Public Library

16 Atlantic Steamer Fire Company No. 1

17 Oyster Bay Post Office

18 Nobman's Hardware Emporium

19 The WaterFront Center

20 Christ Church

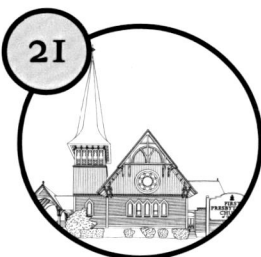

21 First Presbyterian Church

22 Oyster Bay High School

23 Two by Four

24 Derby Hall Bandstand

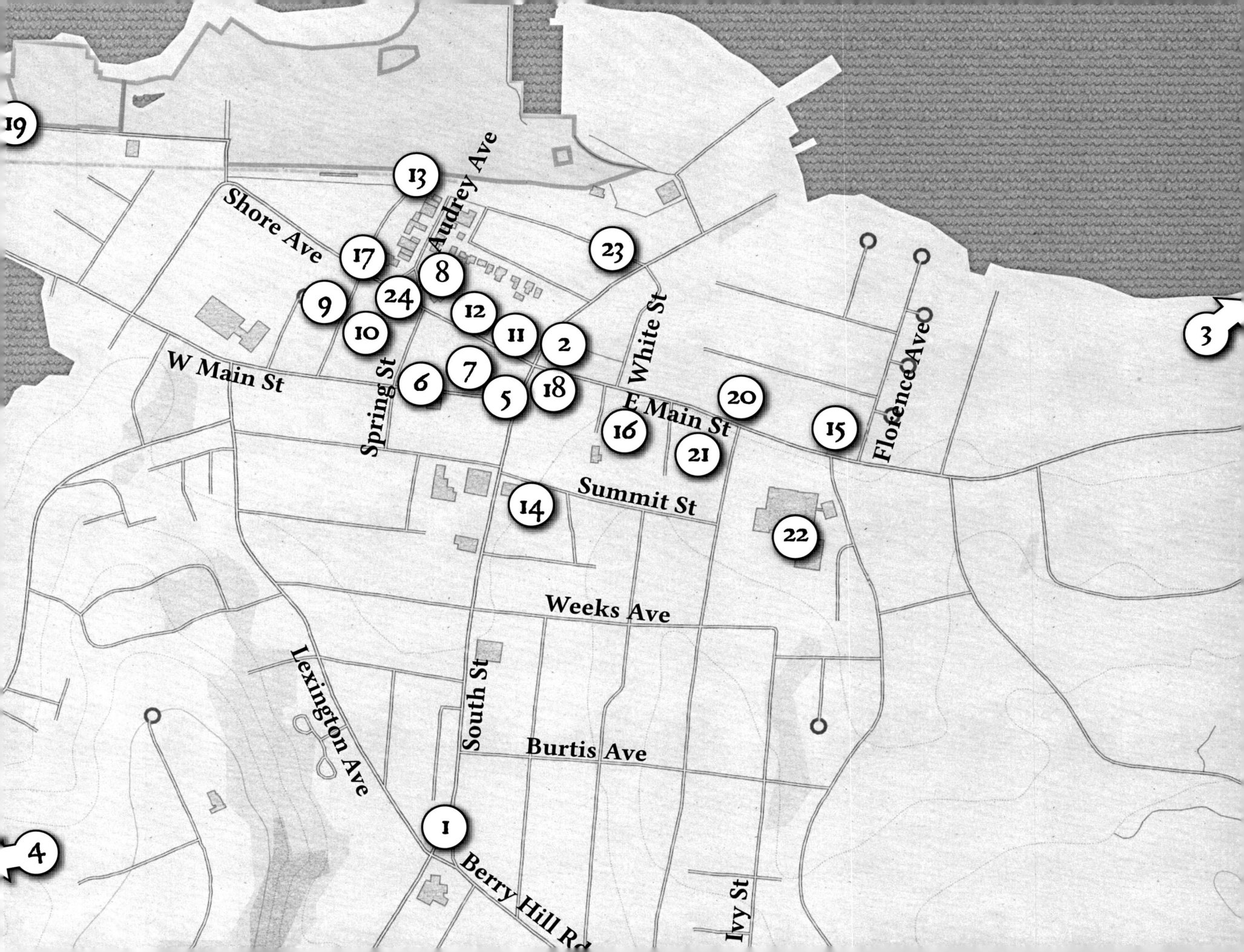

Audrey Ave

Shore Ave

White St

Spring St

W Main St

E Main St

Florence Ave

Summit St

Weeks Ave

Lexington Ave

South St

Burtis Ave

Ivy St

Berry Hill Rd

19

13

17   8

23

9   24   12

10   11   2

6   7   18   5

16   20

21   15

14

22

1

4

3

1.
THEODORE ROOSEVELT STATUE

After five years being in front of the Boys & Girls Club of Oyster Bay, the bronze horseback statue of Theodore Roosevelt was placed in a mini-park at the gateway to the hamlet in 2010, where its supporters always wanted it to be located. In total, Oyster Bay spent over a million dollars in buying the property from Islanders owner Charles Wang, preparing the mini-park, and moving the 2 1/2-ton sculpture to its esteemed location. In addition to the statue, the triangle features five trees, each representing an Oyster Bay resident killed during World War I, including Quentin Roosevelt, a son of the former president. However, that money was well-spent, as the mini-park and statue present a fantastic entrance to the community.

2.
MOORE'S BUILDING/WILD HONEY

Built in 1891 and named after James Moore, the Queen Anne styled Moore Building was expanded in 1901 with the addition of two floors and a corner tower. Included on the National Register of Historical Places, the Building is best known for being where President Theodore Roosevelt's secretary William Loeb, Jr. conducted business when Teddy resided at Sagamore Hill. Legend has it that the first around the world cable transmission was sent from this building by Roosevelt in 1903. Rob and Tina O'Brien bought the building in 2004 and named their restaurant Wild Honey after a U2 song. By serving small and affordable plates, guests can try a variety of Wild Honey's specialties.

3.
SAGAMORE HILL

Sagamore Hill was the home of Theodore Roosevelt, 26th President of the United States, from 1885 until his death in 1919. During Roosevelt's time in office, his "Summer White House" was the focus of international attention. Explore 83 acres of natural surroundings and historic buildings and become inspired by the legacy of one of America's most popular presidents. During his presidency, Sagamore Hill became an important landmark as it served as Roosevelt's "Summer White House." From 1902 to 1908, countless historical events, including visits from foreign dignitaries and talks that would eventually help end the Russian-Japanese War, occurred at Sagamore. This national historic site sits on 83 acres of forest, tidal salt marsh, and bay beach, and the 23-roomed Victorian-styled house is still furnished as it was during Roosevelt's lifetime.

4.
COE HALL

Surviving as a statement about art, architecture, and landscape, Planting Fields is a Gold Coast estate from the 1920s that features 409 acres of greenhouses, rolling lawns, formal gardens, woodland paths, and outstanding plant collections. Landscaped by the Olmsted Brothers and included in the National Register of Historic Places, Planting Fields is one of only a few surviving estates on Long Island with its original acreage intact. Its main attraction is Coe Hall, a 65-room Tudor Revival mansion designed by Alexander Walker and Leon Gillette. Envisioned in 1913 by William and Mai Coe and completed by the Cauldwell-Wingate Company in 1918, the house's interior is a showcase of artistry and craftsmanship and features an American aesthetic through original ironwork commissions by Samuel Yellin and murals painted by Robert Chanler and Everett Shinn.

Photo by Jbabich21

5.
SNOUDER'S CORNER DRUG STORE

Located on South and West Main Streets, Snouder's Corner Drug Store is an Oyster Bay mainstay. Established in 1884, the drugstore was Oyster Bay's oldest operating business and where the town's first telephone was installed. However, the store closed in 2010. Bought by Hamid Nazif in 2015, he had A.S. Engineering Services P.C. evaluate Snouder's in 2017. Stating that the building's condition was poor, they noted that Snouder's be demolished and that a new edifice be built. But in 2019, Tim Lee, a Cold Spring Harbor builder who specializes in historic restoration, and his partners Claudia Taglich and Lenore Mahoney, became the new owners of Snouder's. Snouder's is now undergoing a restoration in a way that celebrates its history.

SNOUDERS
CORNER DRUGSTORE

Photo by idoysterbay

6.
RAYNHAM HALL

Raynham Hall Museum is best known as the home of Robert Townsend, a central member of George Washington's legendary Culper Spy Ring. Robert saw his family's home and his town forcibly occupied by British forces throughout the years of the Revolutionary War. Lt. Col. John Graves Simcoe, commander of the Queen's Rangers, was the most notable unwelcome guest, and stayed in the house during three separate occupations, writing the first known Valentine's poem in America to Robert's sister, Sarah, in 1779. The house and its property had been purchased in 1738 by Robert's father Samuel, an active member of the New York Provincial Congress and outspoken advocate of independence from Britain. Samuel was a successful shipping merchant who lived here with his wife, Sarah, and their eight children, as well as around 20 enslaved people who worked in the fields, the house, and the shipyard. In the 1850s, Samuel's grandson Solomon and his family moved to Oyster Bay from Manhattan, transforming the home into a quintessential Victorian showpiece. The front part of the house was then restored a hundred years later to its previous 18th century appearance, following the discovery that Robert Townsend had actually been undercover agent Samuel Culper, Jr. Today, Raynham Hall Museum receives around 10,000 visitors a year for its Augmented Reality and docent-led tours.

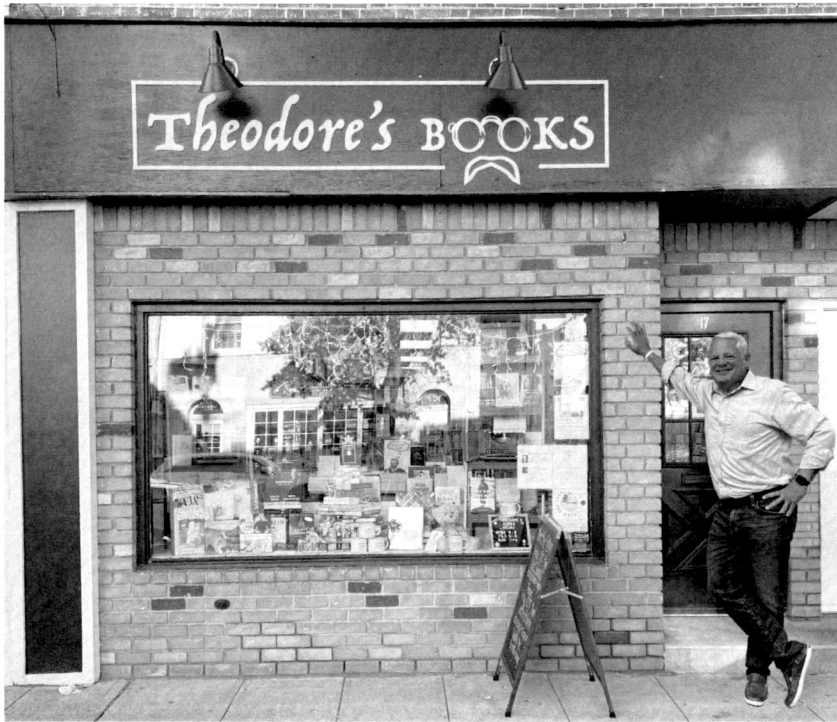

7.
THEODORE'S BOOKS

Offering a wide inventory of new books in Oyster Bay, Theodore's Books creates a warm and friendly place to browse and buy history, current affairs, classic literature, the hottest best-sellers, and beautiful children's titles. They feature an attractive selection of gifts and accessories for book lovers including greeting cards, journals, and puzzles. A dedicated community partner, a destination experience for its customers, and home to a fun and extensive online platform (theodoresbooks.com). Theodore's Books is owned by former Congressman Steve Israel, who decided to turn the page from a career in politics and find a place where there's no screaming, lobbying, or finger-pointing (unless it's the tip of your finger against a line in a book you love).

8. SHOPS OF OYSTER BAY

TABY'S

A classic Greek diner serving breakfast, lunch, and dinner, Taby's has some tasty burgers to offer in a casual setting. If you want the diner experience, breakfast all day, or its Greek specialties, Taby's is your place.

SOUTHDOWN COFFEE

At Southdown Coffee, you can get a great eco-friendly cup of Joe as well as fresh baked goods and made to order sandwiches.

BAHR GALLERY

Ted Bahr promotes and sells beautiful psychedelic posters for you to enjoy in his wide gallery space with stark white walls.

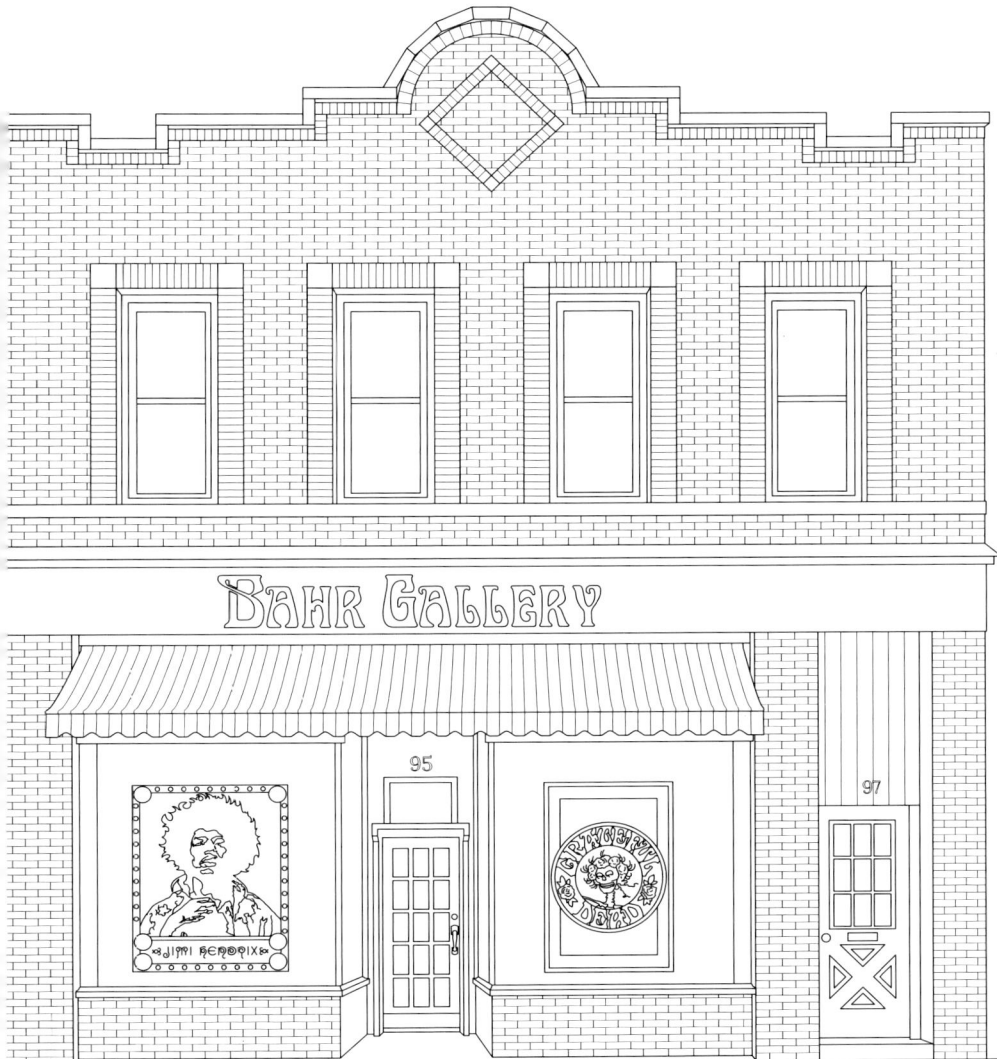

SWEET TOMATO

A family-owned deli famous known for their large selection of delicious soups. Founded in 2004 by Tina Mazarella, Sweet Tomato is run by three generations, led by Diana Trama. Grab a cup of coffee, a sandwich, salad, or cup of soup at Sweet Tomato today.

BAHR GALLERY

95

97

SMOOTHIES WRAPS PANINIS

Sweet Tomato

SALADS SOUPS BAKERY

9.
BONANZA STAND OF OYSTER BAY

A special part of Oyster Bay history is Bonanza Stand, one of the oldest businesses in Oyster Bay. Originally from Italy, John Bonanza came to America to pursue the American dream. His first stop was Canarsie, Brooklyn. In the early 1900's, he and his family relocated to Oyster Bay. Initially just a small pushcart, John sold peanuts, lemon ice, and worms for the fishermen to use as bait at the waterfront. When John later built a stand next to his house, children came to watch him squeeze the lemons and crank the handle on his rock-salt ices machine. 125 years and three generations later, children and adults line up at Bonanza's for great hot dogs, French fries, pretzels, nachos, chicken fingers, onion rings, and a wide variety of delicious Italian ices. Philip Sr. and his wife Patricia still sell the soft clouds of lemon ice made fresh at Bonanza Stand. The lemon ice tastes like frozen fresh-squeezed lemonade with the pits still in it, not too tart and not too sweet. Phil Sr. also does a banner business in all beef hot dogs. The Bonanza Dog is loaded with ketchup, mustard, sauerkraut, relish, onions, cheese and chili. People still come here every single day for a hot dog and the lemon ice.

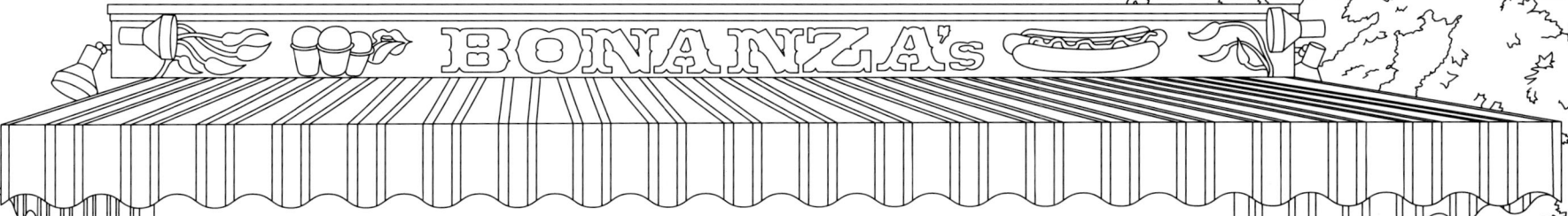

BONANZA's

BONANZA STAND OF OYSTER BAY, NY
Serving Customers For Over 100 Years
MENU

Homemade Italian Ices

Small $	Large
Blue Raspberry	Peanut Butter
	Pina Colada
Cherry	
Chocolate	Rainbow
Chocolate Oreo	Raspberry
Cotton Candy	Strawberry
Lemon	Vanilla Choc Chip
Orange	Pistachio
Orange Cream Delight	
Peach	
Banana Creme	
Bubble Gum	Peanut Butter & Jelly
Cake Batter	Pink Lemonade
Cappuccino	
	Reese's
Coconut	Snickers
Green Mint Chip	
	Sugar Free Cherry
Mango	

Homemade Italian Ices to Go

½ Pint
Pint
Quart
Party Tub   Inquire   Inquire

Hot Dogs - Plain, Mustard
Sauerkraut, Ketchup, Relish
Onion Dog
Cheese Dog
Chili Dog
Bonanza Dog
Hot Dog no Bun
Sloppy Bo (chili on a bun)
Steak Fries Sm
Cheese Fries Sm
Bonanza Fries Sm
Nachos with Cheese
Nachos w/ Chili & Cheese
Onion Rings Sm
Bowl of Homemade Chili
Chicken Tenders
Chicken Wings
Mazzerella Sticks
Potato Chips
Hot Pretzel

Fountain Soda
Small 12oz. $ MeD
Coke, Diet Coke, Root Beer, Sprite,
Orange, Ice Tea
Bottle Drinks
Coke, Diet Coke (20oz.)
Apple Juice
Canned Drinks

Dr. Browns Cream, Black Chrerry $
Bottle Water 16.9oz

BONANZA

SODA

GUSTO

(since) 1897!

quality!

10.
2 SPRING

Created by Claudia and Michael Taglich and Iron Chef winner Jesse Schenker, 2 Spring is an American Brasserie that celebrates the essence of mid-century Manhattan, where well-prepared food was served in settings that were both sophisticated and unpretentious. 2 Spring brings the hospitality and quality of Manhattan's finest downtown eateries to Oyster Bay through a rotating menu of American fare served in a comfortably upscale and established environment, making it the hottest restaurant in town. Located in a building constructed in the 1920s, Jim Smiros and Sophie Thibon created 2 Spring's design scheme. For the restaurant's exterior, the designers kept the original brick work and added gas-style lamps as well as signs for the restaurant. For its interior, the restaurant was given an aged look with a veneered tin ceiling, walls plastered with a brick covering, a hardwood floor, and cloud lighting that used old liquor bottles. To make the building's second floor feel like both a special destination and seamlessly interact with the first floor, the designers created a shaft to connect the first and second floor and enclosed the staircase with glass.

11.
OYSTER BAY BREWING COMPANY

Dedicated to producing the highest quality beer while staying true to their nautical history on the Gold Coast, Oyster Bay Brewing Company is in the business of making great beers locally on Long Island. Since 2012, the brewery has been committed to producing unconventional ales and lagers that defy styles, categories, and your imagination. They take special care to ensure every handcrafted batch is the best they can brew, as their brews utilize only the best ingredients with a sensational rich taste.

12.
TEDDY'S BULLY BAR

Depicting Teddy Roosevelt's face on a glowing neon sign, Teddy's Bully Bar has become an instant hit for Oyster Bay residents. Managed by Angelo Monniello, Teddy's Bully Bar is located on Audrey Avenue in the space formerly occupied by Canterbury's. While Canterbury's was Oyster Bay's most dependable local haunt for decades, the pandemic forced the restaurant to close down, leaving residents with a need for a casually elegant place. Teddy's delivers this desire in spades, by presenting a beautiful dining room with bar tables atop vintage bicycles and a new fireplace to take diners back in time with a modern twist. The menu's highlights include the Hangover, a char-grilled burger topped with a fried egg, bacon, and Cheddar cheese; a panini-style Cuban sandwich of roast pork and Swiss cheese; grilled oysters with bacon, Parmesan cheese, and cherry peppers; and fried codfish.

13.
OYSTER BAY RAILROAD MUSEUM

The Oyster Bay Railroad Museum has as its mission to heighten the public's awareness, understanding and appreciation of the railroad's role and impact on Long Island. It collects, preserves and interprets the Long Island Railroad's heritage for current and future generations. The genesis of the Museum began in 1990, when a group of dedicated volunteers, in an effort to save the retired steam locomotive #35 from a rusty fate, incorporated as the Friends of Locomotive #35. As time went on and the group's efforts were bearing fruit, it became apparent that their focus was greater than the locomotive, and when the Oyster Bay train station (circa 1889) was deactivated and title transferred to the Town, the Oyster Bay Railroad Museum was formed in 2007 with the goal of restoring the station, along with acquiring vintage railroad cars and equipment. The Museum operates on a seasonal basis from the historic station at Railroad Avenue and a Display Yard at Bay Avenue. To learn more about the Museum, visit www.obrm.org and on Facebook.

LONG ISLAND

12

BLT227N52A

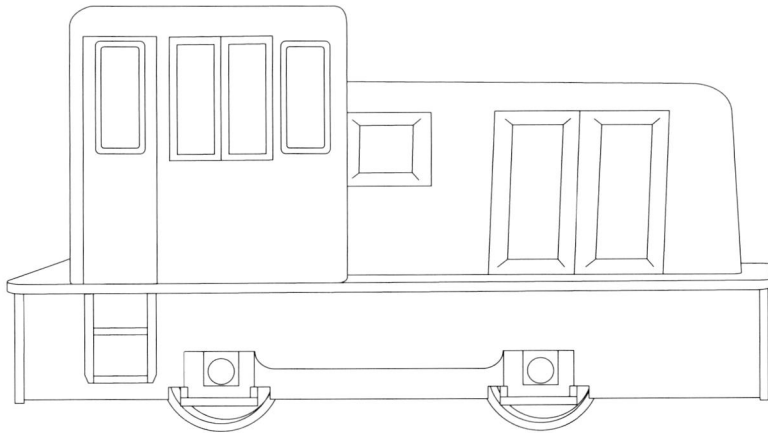

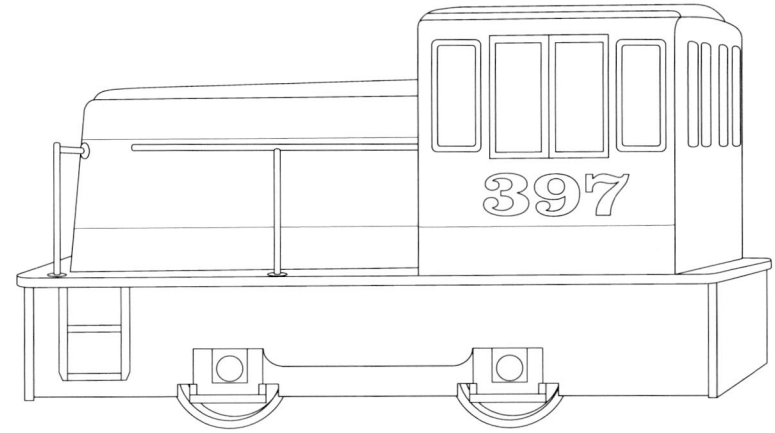

397

7001

14.
OYSTER BAY HISTORICAL SOCIETY

Founded in 1960 and chartered in 1966, the Oyster Bay Historical Society opened in the Wightman House in 1972. The first floor held meeting and reading rooms, exhibition space, a reference library, and a working kitchen. With Thomas Kuehhas' hiring in 1992, the Society reinterpreted the Wightman House's two front rooms as a Colonial living space and a 19th-century minister's parlor respectively, while the North Country Garden Club transformed the back grounds to an 18th-century garden. Opening in 2011, the Koenig Center boasts an exhibit gallery, workshop facilities, a library, a kitchen, and staff offices. However, the Wightman House has not been left behind, as it still features its 18th and 19th century period rooms, a shop dedicated to arts and crafts, and a permanent exhibit on the house's history.

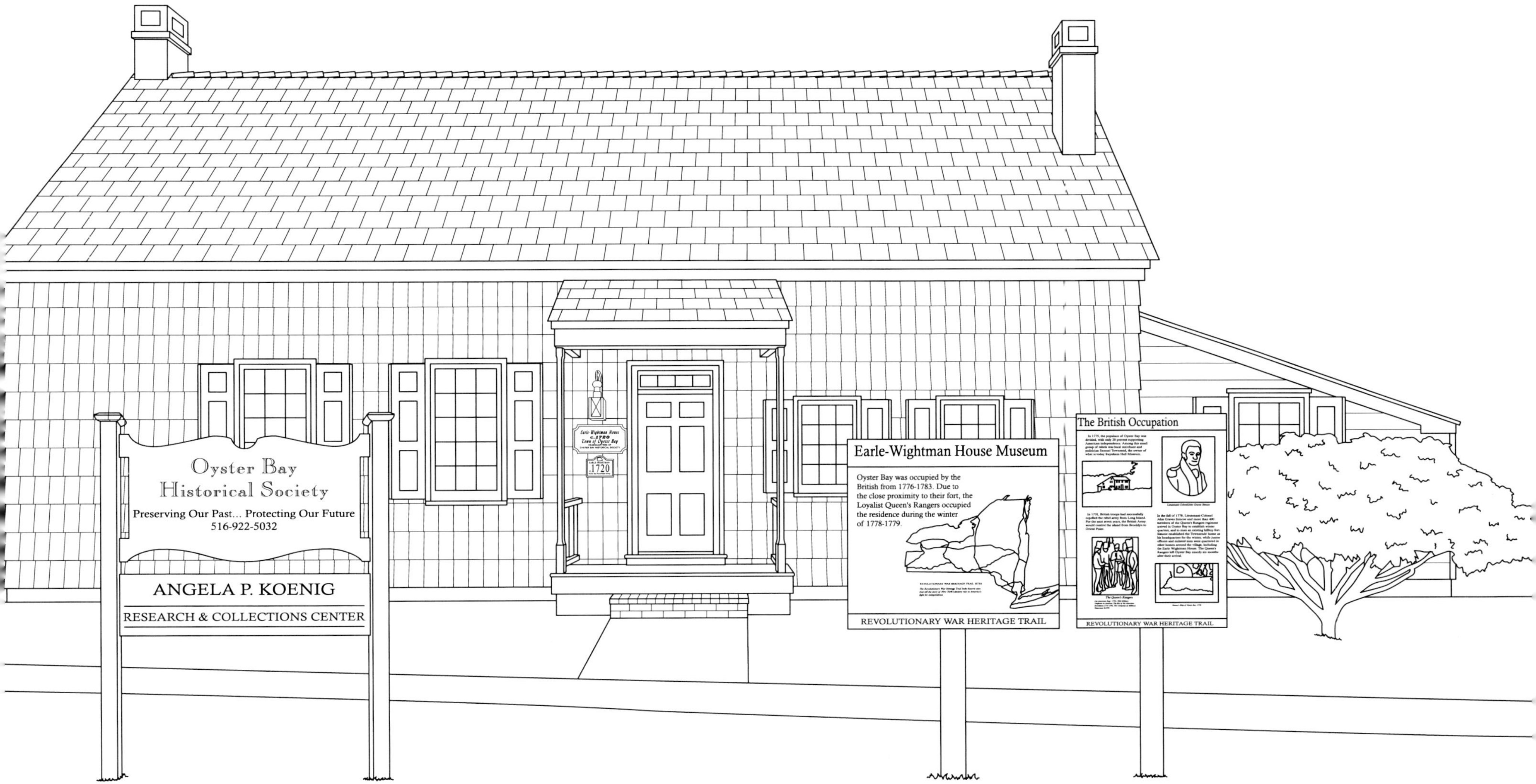

Oyster Bay
Historical Society

Preserving Our Past... Protecting Our Future
516-922-5032

ANGELA P. KOENIG

RESEARCH & COLLECTIONS CENTER

1720

Earle-Wightman House Museum

Oyster Bay was occupied by the
British from 1776-1783. Due to
the close proximity to their fort, the
Loyalist Queen's Rangers occupied
the residence during the winter
of 1778-1779.

REVOLUTIONARY WAR HERITAGE TRAIL

The British Occupation

REVOLUTIONARY WAR HERITAGE TRAIL

15.
OYSTER BAY EAST NORWICH PUBLIC LIBRARY

With a nearly century-long evolutionary process, the Oyster Bay East Norwich Library has had a very unique history. Initially known as the Oyster Bay Free Circulating Library, Governor Theodore Roosevelt laid the library's cornerstone in 1899 and it was dedicated in 1901. Remodeled in memory of Theodore Roosevelt, Jr. in 1949, the Oyster Bay Library eventually merged with the East Norwich Public Library (which was founded in 1938). In 1967, the State Education Department issued a Charter to Oyster Bay – East Norwich Public Library. The Bishop House was bought in 1974 and was renovated the following year. A Non-Fiction area and a Community Room were added in 1981 and 1984, respectively. The library undertook a major renovation and expansion project in the early 1990's, with the building reopening in 1993 and the project being completed in 1994.

Oyster Bay – East Norwich

PUBLIC LIBRARY

16.
ATLANTIC STEAMER COMPANY NO. 1

When Atlantic Steamer Fire Company No. 1 was formed in 1890, firefighters used steam instead of pumps to pressurize water, and hoses were wheeled to fires on carts pulled by men running down streets. Over 130 years later, firefighters say the same spirit of volunteerism, a commitment to risk their lives to assist others, and an intense camaraderie continue to imbue the company. Serving Oyster Bay, Oyster Bay Cove, Cove Neck, Laurel Hollow, and Mill Neck, Atlantic Steamer was established when some members from Oyster Bay Fire Company No. 1. wanted to join another company, but organizational issues led them to form their own company. Today the companies complement each other, as Atlantic Steamer has the North Shore's only dive/water rescue team, while Oyster Bay has an ambulance. Atlantic Steamer has about 80 volunteers, including an active core of 26 who dedicate four to five hours a day to the department.

ATLANTIC STEAMER FIRE CO NO. 1

Photo by idoysterbay

17.
OYSTER BAY POST OFFICE

Designed by William Bottomley in 1936, the Colonial Revival styled Oyster Bay Post Office replicates the nearby Oyster Bay Town Hall. Scenes from history are depicted through Ernest Peixotto's murals, and the ceiling has been beautified by Arthur Sturges' depiction of North America receiving mail from women of various nations by planes and ships. Included in the National Register of Historic Places and the Oyster Bay History Walk, the post office contains many examples of New Deal artwork. Ernest Peixotto painted five murals of historic Oyster Bay from 1653 to 1936. The messenger Mercury sits atop the dome to quickly receive the mail. Leo Lentelli created the terracotta panels above the doorways, depicting the continents symbolized by animals. On the Africa/Oceania panel the dates 1858 and 1919 refer to the years of Theodore Roosevelt's life. On the Asia/America panel the date 1902, the year Roosevelt returned to Oyster Bay as President and the year 1936, the year the Post Office was built. Lentelli also sculpted a bust of Theodore Roosevelt, a flagpole base outside the Post Office, and the seahorses, dolphins, and shells you see today.

18.
NOBMAN'S HARDWARE EMPORIUM

Owned and operated by five generations of the Nobman family, Nobman's Hardware Emporium has evolved over the past 100-plus years alongside Oyster Bay to ensure that the community's needs are met by a caring staff and a broad base of quality products. As a full service hardware, home furnishings, and specialty store, Nobman's dedication to providing customers with the highest standard in quality products and personalized service distinguishes the store from any other retail experience on Long Island. Founded in 1910 by William and Frederick Nobman, Nobman's is imbued with a sense of history and continuity to the area's residents while also looking forward to serving its customers for the next 100 years.

19.
WATERFRONT CENTER

Established in 2000, The WaterFront Center is a non-for-profit organization providing access to the waters of Oyster Bay Harbor and Long Island Sound through their marine education programs, recreational and instructional sailing programs, paddleboard, kayak and sailboat rentals, and through harbor tours aboard the National Historic Landmark oyster sloop CHRISTEEN. Each year, they provide engaging hands-on activities to more than 20,000 students, families, veterans, and people with disabilities to help them learn about and appreciate the marine environment. The WaterFront Center's mission is to connect people to the water through education and recreation utilizing Beekman Beach, West Harbor, and the surrounding ecosystems as outdoor classrooms where learning knows no bounds. From their signature events to their core programs, The WaterFront Center strives to build a community of stewards for the environment who will ensure that Oyster Bay and its resources are available for generations to come.

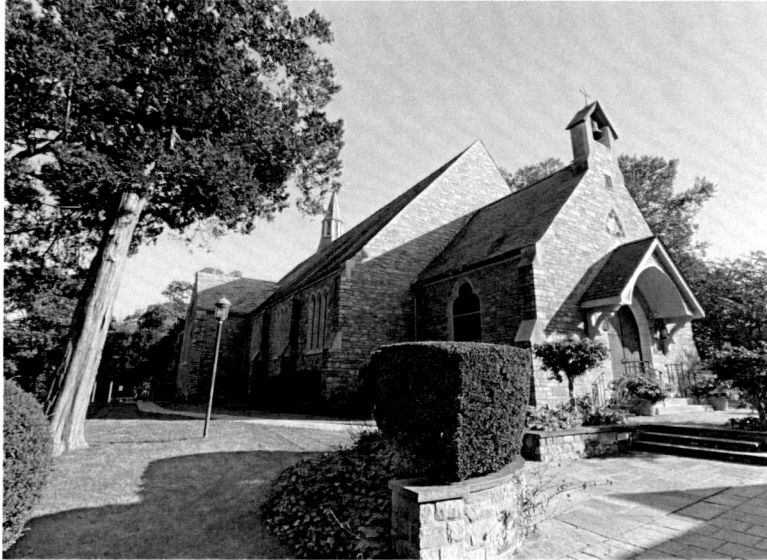

Photo by idoysterbay

Photo from Christ Church Oyster Bay

20.
CHRIST CHURCH

With its roots as a colonial outpost for the Church of England, Christ Church has had a fascinating history since it was established in 1705. Over its lifespan, Christ Church has functioned in a Town House, a purpose-built church, Oyster Bay Academy (the church's current rectory), and another church before the current church was built in 1878 and encased in stone in 1925. Christ Church's most famous parishioner was President Theodore Roosevelt, whose funeral took place here in 1919. The Roosevelt family members are memorialized on the church's plaques, and the President's pew is marked with an American flag. Listed in the National Register of Historic Places, Christ Church is one of only a few churches in the United States with a history of over 300 years.

Among the church's greatest treasures are its magnificent stained-glass windows. Created nearly a century ago by Oliver Smith, they tell the Bible story in stages from the Old and New Testaments as the viewer moves from the church's back to its front. Inspired by France's Chartres Cathedral, Oliver designed, colored, fired, and assembled the windows in the church's workshop. The three largest windows in the Chancel and Transepts were made in Oyster Bay, while the aisle and porch windows were completed in Smith's Pennsylvania studio.

Christ Church
Founded 1705

21.
FIRST PRESBYTERIAN CHURCH

While the First Presbyterian Church's ministry began in Oyster Bay in 1842, the congregation initially had no permanent church building. The first church building was located on East Main Street at the rear half of the present Nobman's Hardware. In 1872, Pastor Benjamin Swan began designing this church on the hill. Built in 1873 by J. Cleveland Cady, First Presbyterian Church is an historic Carpenter Gothic-style Presbyterian church building located at 60 East Main Street. Dramatic arched entryways inside the church are inscribed with Biblical verses. A Hillborn Roosevelt pipe organ was placed at the front of church. William Swan donated and played the organ for next 52 years. The congregation is noted for its association with Theodore Roosevelt, Sr., his wife Martha Roosevelt, and their children (including their son and future United States president Theodore Roosevelt, Jr.). Theodore Roosevelt, Sr's funeral was held in this building in 1878. In 1976, the church building was added to the National Register of Historic Places.

FIRST
PRESBYTERIAN
CHURCH
of Oyster Bay

22.
OYSTER BAY PUBLIC SCHOOL

Designed by Tooker & Marsh in 1928, the four story Oyster Bay High School incorporates the forms and details of the Tudor, Gothic, Art Deco, and Beaux arts styles. A central three bay, four story section is flanked by symmetrical pairs of five bay wings which in turn are flanked by bookend sections. Throughout the façade, stone blocks cap the brick piers that divide each bay section from another. Below the parapet is a stone frieze with Gothic detail. A mock vaulted ceiling covers the vestibule. Inside, the main auditorium has Gothic details including diamond paned leaded windows, Tudor type wall paneling, stucco and stone quoined walls, and a pair of tabernacle canopies that flank a decorated proscenium.

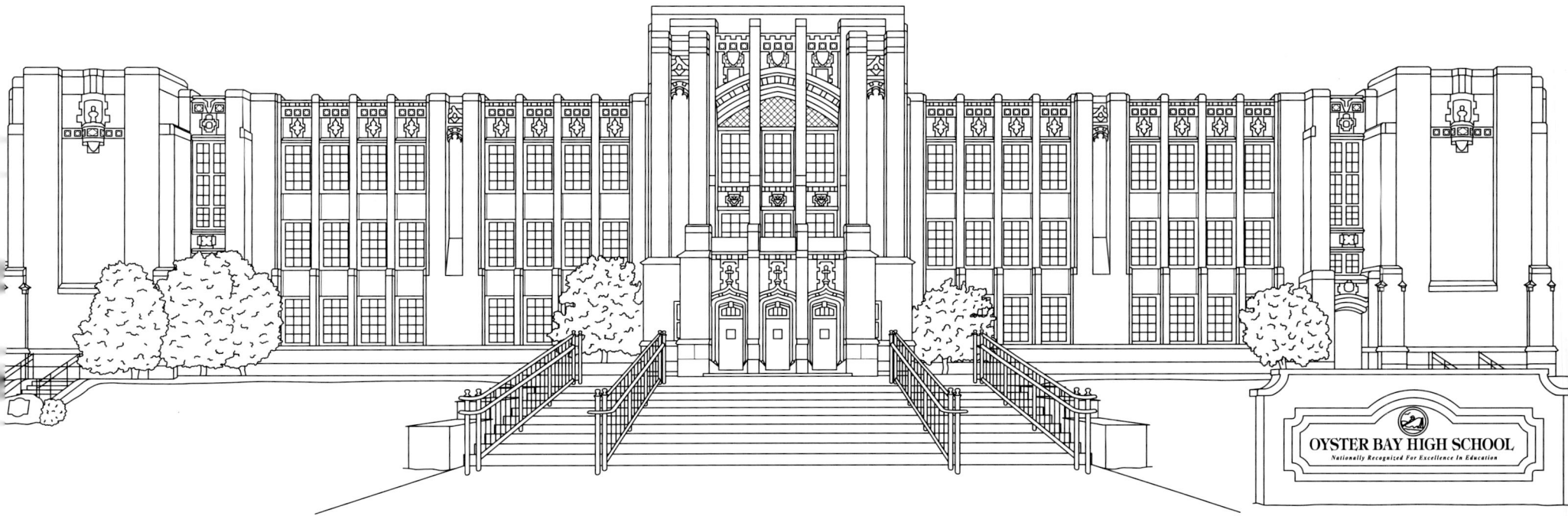

OYSTER BAY HIGH SCHOOL

Nationally Recognized For Excellence In Education

Photo from Two by Four Instagram

23.
TWO BY FOUR

Welcome to your pet's paradise...where you can trust trained staff to take the utmost care of your furry-family members. Whether you are at work for the day, away for a weekend, or gone for a few months - they have created the perfect home away from home for your pets by showering them with love, introducing them to new pup-friends, and allowing them to have endless amount of time outside in the fresh air. They specialize in socializing your pup and pride themselves on their indoor/outdoor facility and have tons of activities to entertain even the most energetic pup. Started in 2007, a small dog-walking service was quickly built into a pet empire as Long Island's Premier dog-walking and doggie daycare service. This is the one-stop shop for all of your pets needs - they can train 'em, clean 'em, feed 'em, and love 'em. This is a true family-run business, and they focus on making both the owner and your furry-family member feel as if they are at their home away from home!

the Green Acres of OB
at Two By Four NY

24.
DERBY HALL BANDSTAND

Located on Audrey Avenue and Shore Avenue, the Oyster Bay Derby Hall Bandstand is a replica of the one that stood 100 years ago. One of the first structures built along Audrey Avenue, the bandstand was used by President Theodore Roosevelt to give his public speeches. Today, the bandstand remains as a gathering place on holiday occasions like the 4th of July parade and festivities. The bandstand is surrounded by three cannons: one of which has a tablet fixed to it that was cast from metal recovered by the *U.S.S. Maine* destroyed in 1898. Another cannon has a plaque that reads "Civil War Trophy Gun...Made in 1861...Unveiled By Theodore Roosevelt President of United States June 27, 1903."

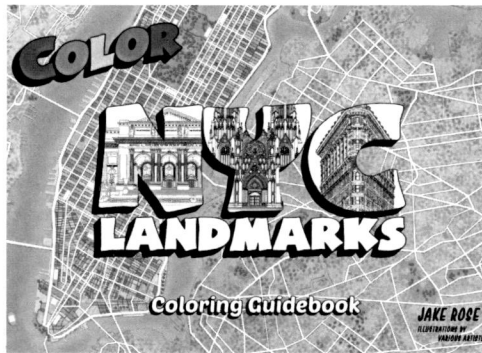

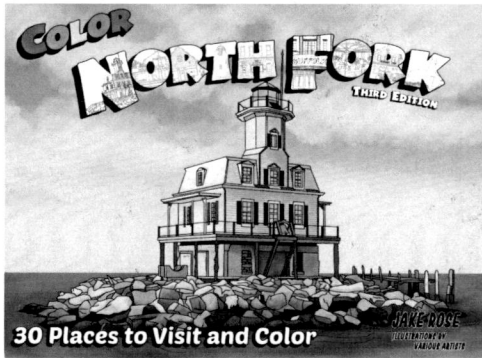

With a degree in history, Jake Rose pursues his passion for architecture, photography, and most importantly, historic landmarks.

Jake honors Oyster Bay's unique historical institutions in his signature style. Collaborating with artists around the world, beautiful line drawings are created using Jake's own photographs, which are each accompanied by a rich detailed history which makes it unique in the world of coloring books.

The newest edition in the "Color Our Town" series, "Color Oyster Bay" celebrates the multitude of the town's most noted attractions.

Visit Jake at ColorOurTown.com,
and on Instagram and Facebook @colorourtown